ROGER EMERSON

SiNG
6 - 7 - 8 !

50 WAYS TO IMPROVE YOUR ELEMENTARY OR MIDDLE SCHOOL CHOIR

HAL•LEONARD®

Published by Hal Leonard Corporation
7777 W. Bluemound Road
P.O. Box 13819
Milwaukee, WI, 53213

Library of Congress Cataloging-in-Publication Data

Emerson, Roger.
   Sing 6-7-8! : 50 ways to improve your elementary or middle school choir / by Roger
Emerson ; edited by Sharon Stosur.
      p. cm.
   ISBN 978-1-4234-5479-3
   1. Choral singing--Instruction and study--Juvenile. I. Title. II. Title: Sing six-seven-
eight!
   MT915.E44 2008
   782.5071'2--dc22

                                        2007051754

Printed in the U.S.A.

Visit Hal Leonard Online at www.halleonard.com

FOREWORD

I don't know about you, but I am forever skipping the foreword of any book so that I can get right into the real meat of the text. I'm hoping, however, that this time you will take a few minutes to read this forward because it is very important to understanding the essence of the book that follows.

Let me begin by saying that this book is geared towards the non-select ensemble, better known as the "y'all come" choir. It should be helpful for the inexperienced teacher or band director who is just starting out, as well as for the experienced teacher who is looking for some new approaches and ideas. It is not a comprehensive method, but rather a survival guide. I feel strongly that middle school singers are very talented, full of ability and energy, and that once harnessed and directed, can be quite satisfying musically. I also believe that anyone who can successfully teach middle school choir can probably teach just about anything, including all other levels of choral music.

As many of you perhaps, I never intended to teach middle school music. I was sure that I wanted to teach high school or college, and mentally prepared myself to do so. But my first five years were spent teaching K-8 general, instrumental, and vocal music. Interestingly enough, I graduated as an applied vocal major, and was much more concerned about my ability to teach band than choir. Even more interesting is that my bands consistently received Superior I ratings, while my choirs only received Excellent II and Good III ratings in the early years.

I have done a great deal of retrospective analysis as to why this was so, and I have made the following observations. 1. Instrumental music was my weaker area and I worked harder at its instruction 2. Instrumental music traditionally uses a sequential method (a band book) that insures that posture, breathing, tone, articulation, and reading music are reinforced. 3. The literature for instrumental music is carefully graded according to experience and ability level. 4. Playing an instrument is not as closely tied to the students' self-image and confidence level and therefore an easier "sell."

As I said earlier, I spent my first five years building a program in which many students participated, and I trust most of them enjoyed the experience. My bands were musically literate and played quite well. My choirs, although popular, were not particularly literate, nor did they sing with much beauty, grace, balance or blend. It was not something that I was particularly proud of, but I really didn't know how to make it happen. I went on to teach at higher levels with varying degrees of success, but it always haunted me that I had not done justice to those middle school singers.

After a ten year hiatus from teaching in which I focused on writing, arranging, listening and learning about choral performance, I returned to the middle school choral classroom when my own children were entering 6th grade. Our local middle school of about three hundred students had lost its music program, and I wasn't about to let my own daughters go through their school years without music. I vowed that this time I would do a better job of teaching choral music. I had learned a great deal listening, watching and analyzing what the best choral directors in the country were doing, and I had the privilege of access to many choral masters such as Rodney Eichenberger, Charlene Archibeque, Howard Swan, Henry Leck and others, and I was anxious to put what I had learned into action.

The handbook that follows is the result of those successful years when my average choir became an award-winning one. I have made an effort to succinctly illustrate the processes and techniques used to get there, and have written in an easy question and answer format. In most instances I have given the simple, straight-forward answer as I see it, and I have also suggested additional sources for a more in-depth look or exercise on the topic. The questions and answers are in random order, and there is some overlap in that most problems are corrected by attention to, or systematic application of the basics. I hope that the ideas presented here will work for you as well as they have for me.

Roger Emerson, January 2008

1

Q. I only have a few students in my choir. How do I build the numbers?

A. There are several factors that can affect the size of your choir, and I will try to address several of them. If the ensemble is new, or you are new to the program, it will take a year or so to see a measurable difference. The history and perception of the choir in your school is a big factor in its popularity. Let's face it, you may have to do quite a bit of cheerleading at first to bring students into the program. Often times just an invite in the hallway will result in a new member. *Recruit the popular students by making a connection with them.* Go to their sports events and let them know how much you admire their athletic ability. All it takes is a few well-liked students in your program before others will follow. *Perform a wide variety of music from edited classics to the latest pop tune.* Feature individual young men and women on specific numbers. Hold a talent contest. Put on a "pop" musical. Add a local garage band to a number or program. *Make your classroom the place to be,* a place where students and their ideas are valued. Never embarrass your musicians by performing music that is not ready, or inappropriate for their age. Remember that middle school students exist in that weird place between childhood and adulthood. Err on the side of treating them more like adults. Build a quality program and "they will come." Kids, all of us for that matter, are attracted to quality and want to be a part of something perceived as good.

A true story: When I went back to teaching, our middle school had started a new "elective" choir program and only seventeen students showed up for the first meeting. Needless to say, I was devastated because my choirs had always had at least fifty students. For a fleeting second I considered turning the ensemble into a guitar class where size did not matter. Then (thank goodness) I regained my senses and realized that these seventeen students wanted to sing MORE than any other elective activity. I was suddenly reenergized and decided to move ahead with my plans for uniforms, festival participation and a tour to the Bay Area where we would perform for other middle schools and conclude with a day at a theme park. Needless to say, it wasn't long before word got around about the exciting activities the choir had planned. Second quarter we grew to thirty-five, and completed the year at fifty students. BUILD IT AND THEY WILL COME!

2

Q. Many of my boys cannot match pitch. What can I do?

A. It is important to remember that in singing, the boys are often several years behind the girls in experience. As infants girls are sung to and expected to sing back, but the same is not always true for boys. If we sang to young men as often as we put a ball in their hands, matching pitch when they reach school age would not be a problem. When they reach school age there is sometimes the stigma that singing is not masculine, or the range of classroom songs is too high to be comfortable. Either way, some boys just stop, or never even start using their vocal instrument. Boys who sing in grades three, four and five will not have difficulty singing in grades six, seven and eight.

Here are some ideas for helping your young men. *Set aside some time to work with them alone or in small groups,* even if it is that precious five minutes at the beginning or end of the rehearsal. It is critical to determine which boys are having trouble and to assess which notes, if any, they can vocalize. The easiest way, and one that causes the least embarrassment, is to have the young men (five or six at a time), gather around the piano with their backs to the remainder of the choir. Play and sing a simple melodic motive such as "We Will Rock You" starting on Eb above middle C for unchanged voices, or Bb below middle C for changed or changing voices. Move this motive up and down to determine where they start to lose notes. Ultimately, you want to keep a record of each boy's range, as it will change. I always encourage my young men to extend their range up and down. As I tell them, "The guy with the most notes wins!" (You can make the same challenge to the girls so that they also believe a wide range is a virtue.)

Find each boy's pitch. If you encounter a "grumbler" who doesn't seem to be making any sustained pitch at all, make sure that he is filling with air and then have him "sigh" or "hum-siren" as if he has just spotted a big juicy steak or piece of pie. Then find this pitch on the piano and use it as the basis for "Shake, Rattle and Roll" while you play a boogie woogie blues progression with his pitch as the tonic. Get all of the guys to sing along. Then transpose up a step. Before long he will be matching pitches. As I said earlier, he just hasn't used the instrument enough to coordinate what he is hearing with what he is singing.

Use the crank to raise the pitch. Rod Eichenberger advocates using an imaginary "crank" at about belt high. From the lowest pitch the student starts on, crank him up and let the pitch rise to the desired note. *Try falsetto.* Henry Leck has found that some students can match pitch in falsetto easier than full voice. Try a little of "The Lion Sleeps Tonight" starting on D above middle C.

Fully support with prepared air. Make sure the students are taking a full breath and then using the air they have inhaled. Often students will inhale only to trap the air and then try to sing. I believe many non-singers are just not putting enough air through the vocal chords to result in a sustained pitch. Try lip buzzes. Then lip buzzes with pitch. You can't do this without sufficient air connection.

Don't let them continue to grumble (sing low). As boys mature, they want to sing low because it feels more masculine, but once I have them matching pitch in the 6th grade, (often about the same mezzo range as the girls), I encourage them to retain the upper notes while adding notes to the lower range. Remember, the *guy with the most notes wins!*

Occasionally you will also have girls who have not used their voice much and have trouble matching pitch as well. You can use similar exercises with them in a mezzo range.

A true story: I don't believe that there are many non-singers in this world, only those who have not been given the chance to sing under the right circumstances. To illustrate this point, and to share a bit of my naiveté during my first year of teaching, I want to tell the following true story.

In my first year of teaching, I made the terrible mistake of having my 5th grade students audition before they could join choir, only to find that about fifteen of them could not match pitch, boys and girls! Several parents were very upset with my decision and took me before the school board. In order to placate them, I agreed to meet with these students during lunch two days a week. Oddly enough, I called it the non-singing choir! Surprisingly, after about six weeks of singing simple unison songs in a moderate range they all were able to match pitch and I reintegrated them with the other students. The point is, it is usually lack of singing experience in the lower grades that causes problems at the middle school level. Even boys whose voices change at puberty should not have a radical change in ability if they have continued to sing through elementary school. They may lose a few notes for a few weeks but it should not be drastic.

Additional resources:

The Boy's Changing Voice, DVD. Henry Leck. Hal Leonard Corporation.

Enhancing Musicality through Movement, VHS/DVD. Rodney Eichenberger. Santa Barbara Music Publishing, Inc.

Strategies for Teaching Junior High and Middle School Male Singers. Terry Barham. Santa Barbara Music Publishing, Inc.

Success for Adolescent Singers, DVD, Patrick K. Freer, Ed.D., Choral Excellence Inc.

3

Q. My girls have trouble singing anything above C in the staff. How can I get them to vocalize above that pitch?

A. I had the same problem when I started teaching and it was because I allowed them to sing exclusively in chest voice. *Encourage the use of head voice.* It is essential to use warm-ups that will move your singers into the head voice, and then apply those techniques whenever the voice moves into the upper portion of the staff. Purposeful warm-ups that expand the range and tone of our singers may be the most important part of the rehearsal. It is so important that we use the warm-up to increase our singers' range and get them to experience and use the chest, mid-voice and head voice. They will never sing in tune or with beautiful tone above B in the staff if they do not rollover into the lighter head voice.

Try this illustration. For years I have used a simple but effective exercise that, although not politically correct, gives them the sensation of the head voice. Ask the students to repeat after you, in your mid-voice, spoken: "May I please have a glass of milk." And then, in a light heady voice, spoken: "I'd really like a glass of champagne." Finally, in a chesty voice: "Give me a (root)beer!" Tell them you seldom want to hear their "(root)beer" voice, most notes in the staff are sung with the "milk" voice, and to roll into the light head voice at about C in the staff. You can even start to lighten at B.

Another technique is to use the "Mrs. Doubtfire" voice. Most students have seen the movie. If not, show excerpts. It features Robin Williams imitating a kind, elderly woman. This really works well for changed males as well. In addition, you will need to remind them to fully support the sound with air, and to "place" high and light notes which occur in the top part of the staff and beyond. In your warm-up, vocalize up to about C above the staff with nice light, staccato passages, or descending, legato "ee-oo" passages.

Additional resources:

Building Beautiful Voices. Paul Nesheim and Weston Noble. Roger Dean Publishing.

Choir Builders. Rollo Dilworth. Hal Leonard Corporation.

Daily Workout for a Beautiful Voice, VHS/DVD. Charlene Archibeque and Charlotte Adams. Santa Barbara Music Publishing, Inc.

Ready, Set, Sing! VHS/DVD. Jeff Johnson. Santa Barbara Music Publishing, Inc.

4

Q. Several of my singers, especially boys, keep playfully pushing and shoving one another during rehearsal. Do I have to kick them out?

A. One of the first things that I do with a choir is to *give them space*. While standing, have your students put their hands on their hips, spread out until their elbows just touch, then drop hands. This is the minimum distance between each singer. Alternate rows of odd and even numbers of students, and place adjacent rows in the "windows;" the spaces between each student in the row ahead. Not only will students not be inclined to push or shove, but they will develop independent singing and the sound of the choir also will be more open. This is an old Rod Eichenberger technique that is easy to do and works beautifully.

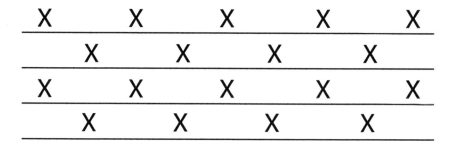

Singing in choir is not for everyone. Some students, especially boys, may feel that the endeavor is too "sissy," or that the idea of public performance is embarrassing. *Make sure that they really want to be in choir.* Once the students are there it is your responsibility to keep the rehearsal moving. It is fatiguing, but you must stay ahead of the students. When rehearsing parts, I would often snap the beat, have one section sing the four or eight-measure phrase, then add the additional parts one at a time without missing a beat. This forces each section to stay engaged and to be ready for their entrance.

If all else fails, *speak with them individually and privately.* Don't put the entire ensemble through a tirade intended for just a select few. Politely ask to see the offenders briefly after class and ask them if they really want to be part of the ensemble. Move them to a different location within the choir if needed. Removing students is always a last resort. Our job is to keep them engaged and educated in the choral art if at all possible. It's also important to remember that some of the worst behaved students need to be part of our choral family even more than many others.

Additional resources:

Best Friends, Worst Enemies. Michael Thompson. Ballentine Books.

The Pressured Child. Michael Thompson. Ballentine Books.

Raising Cain, Protecting the Emotional Life of Boys. Dan Kindlon and Michael Thompson. Ballentine Books.

5

Q. Money to purchase music is always an issue. How can I afford to buy one copy for every student?

A. I often find that administrators will meet our needs if we show them a well thought out plan for expenditures. *Submit a budget for printed music.* It is easy to draw an analogy with textbooks. Most curricular areas receive a new textbook costing around sixty to seventy-five dollars every five years. Music is your textbook! Hence an equitable amount would be fifteen dollars per year, per choir member. This should purchase about eight new pieces of music each year. If all else fails, *put on a musical or talent show* at the beginning of the school year. The proceeds can fund your entire year of new music. Often, if needed, you can borrow money up front from the student body fund to get rolling in the fall.

Seek out a sponsor. Some schools have had success getting businesses or parents to sponsor a song. A sponsorship can be given by a parent as a birthday present if desired.

Consider a "lab" fee. If your school allows a lab fee for classes such as woodshop or science, initiate one for music and let the students keep their folder at the end of the year. Think of the great memories and opportunities for continuing the musical experience as the student grows older. You retain a copy or two and request a reprint from the publisher if the piece goes out of print the next time you want to program the selection. It sure cuts down on storage as well!

I am always very careful about my music purchases. I opt for editions of classics, folk songs and spirituals, several timeless Broadway selections, medleys or classic pop selections, and only an occasional current "pop" song. Rarely can a contemporary pop song be used in subsequent years. My purchases are much like a food pyramid with lasting literature comprising the bulk.

6

Q. I have five boys and thirty girls in my choir. How can I achieve a good balance?

A. *Look for 2-part selections with a moderate part II.* In a 6th grade ensemble, most of the boys will still be comfortable in the part II or alto range, so at that level it is not a problem having them join the girls. However, over time you will need more young men for 3-part mixed or SAB selections in the 7th and 8th grades.

At the 7th and 8th grade level, it does not take very many boys on a well written part to balance the lightness of the females. *Three-part mixed only requires about a 3/3/1 ratio.* Six to eight young men can easily balance fifteen sopranos and fifteen altos.

Consider numbering your singers from low to high instead of labeling them soprano, alto, and baritone. If you have a choir of fifty, give the lowest, darkest voice the number one, and the highest, lightest voice the number fifty. You can then divide them as needed on each part. This really works well on music that is designated with Roman numerals I, II, III. This numbering approach was pioneered by Weston Noble for collegiate ensembles, but it works equally well at the grade school level.

Additional resource:

Up Front! Becoming the Complete Choral Director. Guy B. Webb. E.C. Schirmer Music Company.

7

Q. How do I recruit more boys into my program?

A. It amazes me how some directors just naturally attract young men, and though it is hard to quantify why, here are some ideas. *Let your personality show.* Students immediately sense whether or not you are being your true self, and if you like them and have their best interest at heart. You can't fake it. I often begin the year by telling my students that I love music, and I care about them. That I don't know it all, but that we will learn together. I also promise to make every effort to never embarrass them. If singing a particular piece makes them uncomfortable or is not ready for performance, I'll pull it.

Make sure that the music you choose does not emasculate the boys. No self respecting young man wants to sing about clouds and rainbows. Look for non-gender texts, accompaniments that are strong, rhythmic and often in a minor mode. I always try to grab the guys in the introduction with masculine-sounding chord progressions and rhythms.

Find a song that you can feature them on such as a unison version of "Poison Ivy" or "Rock Around The Clock." Have them wear dark glasses and slick their hair 50's style to be cool. In addition, uniforms should not be feminine colors or styles. Black slacks with shirts and ties, vests or matching golf shirts work well at this level.

Attend athletic events. Tell the athletes what a great job they did at the last game. Once you get a starting center in your choir, the others will follow! If all else fails, grab them in the hall. Not literally, but if you just show some interest and tell them you really need more guys to balance out some very neat girls, they may just decide to join.

Sponsor a battle of the grunge bands. *You may be surprised at the number of talented students in your school who are not involved in traditional music programs.* A healthy relationship with an adult is what all young people are looking for. We offer that on a daily basis in our music programs.

A true story: Let me tell you about Margaret Haggard. She was the quintessential middle school music teacher. Vibrant, energetic, upbeat, unflappable and perfectly coiffed! I met her in the early 1980's at the Choral Arts Seminar of the Rockies in Colorado. She taught just outside Denver and asked me if I would come in and clinic her students. The first thing I noticed was the joy in her classroom. Obviously the students reflected her enthusiasm. I asked, "Where did you get all of these boys"? She simply said, "I just grab them in the hallways and tell them how much we need them!" This was her secret, and I don't think anyone could say no to that fireball of a teacher. She is now retired but I receive her yearly Christmas card with much anticipation and fondness for the vibrant, energetic, upbeat, unflappable and probably still perfectly coiffed, Margaret Haggard!

8

Q. My altos have trouble holding their part and often gravitate to the melody. How do I prevent this?

A. Many girls prefer to sing the alto part because high notes scare them. Let's face it, at the middle school level almost all female singers are mezzo sopranos. One of the first things that I do is make sure that all of the girls vocalize in all registers. I also look for arrangements that give the melody to the altos (part II) some of the time. I then show my enthusiasm for harmony parts, and indicate that it takes a particular talent to sing these parts. I will often *encourage instrumentalists* (students who study piano or play in the band or orchestra) *to sing harmony parts.*

Basic sight-singing is essential. They can't hold the part because they can't read it. We must take five minutes or so of every rehearsal to teach basic sight singing skills. I list a few of my favorite sources in question 45, but you can also create basic scale and intervallic exercises as part of the daily warm-up if desired.

Switch parts on alternating songs. This would be in the best musical interest of all. We don't do it because it requires more time, but it would result in sopranos who hear harmony, and altos who have an extended range. A question that I often pose to music teachers is this, "How would you teach differently if you never had to perform?" The answers are, as you would expect, "I'd teach sight reading. I'd let more students try out for solos. I'd improvise. I'd let all of the students try out the drum set." My suggestion is to perhaps do one less number at the spring concert, and use the resulting extra class time to build musicianship in your students. Teach them to fish – don't just throw them a fish.

Additional resources:

Choir Builders. Rollo Dilworth. Hal Leonard Corporation.

The Choral Approach to Sight Singing. Joyce Eilers and Emily Crocker. Hal Leonard Corporation.

Patterns of Sound. Joyce Eilers and Emily Crocker. Hal Leonard Corporation.

Sing on Sight. Audrey Snyder. Hal Leonard Corporation.

9

Q. All my students want to do is sing "pop" music. How do I get them to sing other types of literature?

A. *"Don't judge a song until you have learned and performed it,"* is a statement my good friend, Greg Eastman tells his students and it seems to work as he has one hundred seventy-five elective singers in a school of four hundred! People would be surprised that even though I make my living writing and arranging mostly pop-style chorals, only about twenty percent of my programming was "pop" in nature. I found that performing quality traditional literature was just as engaging, and "wore" better than most popular songs. In fact, most students prefer the "classic" pieces after they have learned them. I always shared with my students the method to my madness and that I wanted them to experience a balanced diet of songs. We would always perform one of the latest or timeless classic "pop" songs as part of the program, but in addition would perform a folk song or spiritual, a masterpiece, and a composed selection (contemporary festival) at each concert.

You may prefer to save pop style arrangements for the spring concert or end of year "Pops" concert. You can also host a talent show if desired. Also let them know that this IS Choir. Many pop songs do not lend themselves to a choral treatment.

Find quality pieces. The key is finding great pieces that engage the students, and in which the voice leading is logical and makes the piece really "sing." Some compositions and arrangements are just better than others. I have included some lists of my favorites in questions 43, 44 and 45, but ask fellow teachers, your music dealer, etc. Attend "tried and true" sessions often hosted by ACDA or MENC. Find out what the best sellers have been over the years in each of the above categories. One hundred thousand singers cannot be wrong about "The Rhythm of Life," "Ave Verum Corpus" or "Didn't My Lord Deliver Daniel."

A true story: Early in my career I was seated at the head table during a luncheon in which noted choral conductor Howard Swan was the guest speaker. I had been publishing for a few years and had given a workshop on choosing middle school music. Howard's topic was "Choosing Quality Literature," and he began his speech with these words, "Even Bach, Handel, Mozart and (looking over at me) Emerson had their "dusty" pieces!" Everyone, of course laughed. It was a great icebreaker, but more important was the lesson learned. Some pieces are better than others, and even the great composers (of which I don't consider myself), have their weaker compositions. Pick the best of Bach, Handel, Mozart and yes, even Emerson for your concerts. The music is your curriculum.

Q. I don't like to use recorded tracks, but many pop songs sound lackluster without them. Do you have any ideas?

A. *Add a simple drum beat.* Many students in your ensemble will discover a natural rhythmic ability if given the chance. Take a rehearsal and let whoever would like to try these simple beats on a kick (bass) drum, hi-hat, snare drum and ride cymbal. Fills are not necessary at this level, just a steady beat. Start with the bass drum part and then add the snare rhythm and complete it by adding the cymbal pattern. If the drum set gets too loud, have the drummer play with brushes or "hot rods" instead of sticks.

Rock beat:

Rock beat

1. Start with just the bass drum figure using the right foot.
2. Add the snare with the left hand on beats two and four.
3 With the high-hat pedal down with the left foot (closed h.h.), play even eighth notes with the right hand stick.

Swing beat:

Swing beat

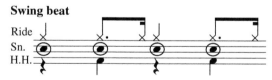

1. Start with the ride cymbal playing the quarter, dotted eighth figure. (Use light 7A sticks or brushes.)
2. Play the hi-hat with the left foot on beats two and four.
3. If using brushes, brush the snare in circles on the beat.

The bass drum is only used occasionally to "kick" into a phrase. With young players it is best to leave it out completely.

Add an electric bass part. Normally the left hand of the piano part in most pop music is a bass part that can be played on a synthesizer or bass guitar. Most modern synthesizers have great sounding acoustic and electric bass samples, and the parts are easy for any middle school student who is taking piano lessons. Chord symbols are provided for those guitar players in your school. They are there-you just have to go after them.

If a guitar player is used, try to keep him or her out of the way of the piano part. If able, he or she should play higher voiced chords if it competes with the piano in the mid-range. Often a simple arpeggiated chord will work well or often short "chunk" chords played on beats two and four will be effective. Sometimes "chorused" whole or half-note chords will provide a wash similar to what I've described below for the electric piano. Listen to what the guitars are doing on the original version of the song.

Add a second keyboard pad. Most pop recordings have a keyboard, such as electric piano, playing "pads." Pads are simply held chords that create a "wash" for the other instruments. You will need to use a little bit of your college theory to write out three or four-note chords from the printed chord symbols for a second keyboard player but it is really worth the time and trouble.

For a final flair, and if you have the aptitude, *add additional instruments such as flute, saxophone or trumpet.* Try your hand at writing easy, unison or octave lines to compliment the voices. Your choir will think they are "big time" when you add simple horn punches to pop music; I know that my students did!

A true story: My college instructor was the well known composer/ arranger, Kirby Shaw. I was a member of his first jazz choir and he always wrote out great horn lines to accompany the voices. When I began teaching middle school, I did the same for my ensembles. Very simple parts made the singers think they were truly professional and the instrumentalists were unusually proud. The importance of keyboard "pads" was learned from my long-time friend (best man at my wedding some twenty-five years ago), arranger and producer Alan Billingsley. When we first met he was producing jingles in Chicago, and I was, in addition to my choral writing, recording original pop songs and trying to get a recording deal. Alan convinced me that I should invest in a home studio, and he would then help me produce my own demos. Sure enough, I did just that and I learned about everything I know about music production from him. Thanks Alan!

11

Q. My singers don't listen to one another and yet I know that it is an important part of choral singing. How do I get them to start listening?

A. Have them consciously listen to another part. I think we assume that our students are listening, but I'm convinced that they are so focused on their own part that they don't listen to those around them. *We need to teach them to listen louder than they sing.* I start by having them listen to just one other part, such as sopranos singing with altos, or altos singing with baritones.

Sing in the round; first in sections and then in a more random formation. You can do this on choral risers by just having them mix up. It's amazing how the blend is improved when you do this. Don't, however, do it too early. Students must be secure with their part before moving out of their section. It also helps to sing the part on a neutral vowel such as "noo."

Use the Socratic Method. I really like what Henry Leck of the Indianapolis Children's Choir does. At the end of a selection he asks these two questions, "What did you think we did well in the performance? What could we do to improve the performance?" This immediately empowers the singers and makes them aware that active listening is an important part of choral singing.

In addition to these ideas, it is so easy to record our ensembles with small digital recorders we should make it a part of our daily rehearsal. Although it is somewhat intimidating, having students sing in trios or quartets will really make singers pay attention. Perhaps you could do it as extra credit so that the uncertain singers are not embarrassed. Or they can record their performance for listening at a later time.

A true story: Singing in a mixed formation is certainly not a new concept, but it may be new to your situation. I know that for many years I just didn't want to take the chance of changing anything for fear I would lose the tenuous stability I was gaining with my 7th and 8th grade chorus. I was so delighted they were singing in tune and could actually produce a well balanced triad the thought of mixing them up was ludicrous. But sure enough, one day (I must have been feeling very confident) I had them stand mixed in a circle to sing a song that we had pretty well together for the concert. It was amazing! Not just the improvement in blend, but the look on their faces when they realized that they could finally really hear one another and that the sound was beautiful. I now do this on a regular basis. Don't be afraid to take that first chance.

12

Q. My principal won't allow our choir to sing any sacred music. How do I convince him or her to change?

A. *Be proactive* by providing your administrator with the rationale for including sacred music in your programs. It's very interesting that in some schools or districts this is not a problem, while in others it's always an issue. I'm convinced that most administrators need to be educated in what we do and why we do it. Almost every statewide ACDA organization has a policy to share with your administrator. Generally the policies ask that we *provide a balanced curriculum* (the sacred material should be offset by similar amounts of secular music), and state that there will be no attempt to evangelize through the music. ICDA (Iowa) policy likens the singing of sacred literature to the study of communism. We study communism but we do not advocate it. The same should be true of singing sacred choral works. *Excluding any one type of music is discriminatory.*

A true story: About ten years ago, my 8th graders wanted to sing "Joyful, Joyful" (the hip version from the movie "Sister Act"), based on Beethoven's "Ode to Joy," at their graduation. It is a very exciting piece and I agreed to teach it to them and direct it. Well, about a week after graduation a parent wrote a letter to the editor in our local paper, upset because of the sacred lyrics. I felt it important to respond, and did so with the following rationale: normally, when our ensemble did a concert, we would present a variety of pieces, however, when we only had the opportunity for one, the result took on the appearance of a skewed program. I felt that its classical roots would be sufficient justification as well. In retrospect, it might have been best to choose something with a secular text, but that is in hindsight. The good news is that the controversy was short lived and has not been an issue since. Very interestingly, I have written several holiday shows that reflect our cultural diversity in this country and the only complaints have been that some administrators won't allow the singing of the "Christian" song. Unfortunately, they are missing the point and that is that we all must be tolerant of differing customs and that to exclude any one type of music is, in fact, discriminatory.

13

Q. What are the most important choral concepts I can teach my choir?

A. Some years ago, having become recently published, I was asked to conduct many regional and county-wide choral festivals. I could always pick out the best choirs simply by the way the students were postured while sitting or standing. Because I was also teaching instrumental music at the time, I began thinking about a systematic approach to teaching singing; similar to the approach we use teaching instrumentalists. A few years later, several publishers created a choral "method" that further reinforced my thinking. Since that time, whenever I work with a choir, PASTA is always my jumping-off point. If an ensemble does not sound good, chances are these principles are not being reinforced. Remember that students bring into the choral rehearsal all of their speaking skills, i.e., poor posture, unprepared air, a horizontal shape, all chest voice and diminished consonants. Singing requires just the opposite and we need to illustrate this.

Posture: I teach my students that they possess a wonderful instrument that must be held properly. In my rehearsals we stand almost exclusively except for occasional part work. I begin by spacing each row. I have them stand with their hands on hips; spread the row until elbows just touch and then drop hands. This is a Rodney Eichenberger technique that opens the sound and encourages singer independence. I then have them raise their hands over their heads and sense the elevation of the rib cage. Keep it there and lower hands. In addition, expand the rib cage up and forward as if the sternum is being reeled in by a fisherman (shoulders pulled back). Feet should be even with shoulders, one foot slightly ahead of the other and hands at side. We never begin singing until the instrument is properly held.

Air: Air is the most vital element of singing and the lack of it the most common reason for intonation and vibrancy problems. I like the idea of filling and expanding the waist area. This encourages low, diaphragmatic breathing. I have students fill for four slow counts and then hiss the air out to a measure of eighth notes and a whole note. What's equally important is to remind them to fill before each and every phrase they sing!

Shape: Uniform vowels lead to beautiful blend. I encourage singers to get out of the horizontal speaking mode and into the vertical singing mode. Drop the jaw and raise the soft palate. (Raised cheek bones and eyebrows help here.) Then we work and look for the shape of each vowel sound, AH, OH (like a smoke ring), Oo (lips puckered), Ee (nice and dark, originating with the Oo with no change in jaw) and Eh not A! I then have students search out these sounds in the lyrics of the song we are about to sing.

Tone: Using this word here is a bit of a stretch. I suppose placement would be a better term but PASPA doesn't work! I try to get students out of the chest and into the head voice by example and the phrase, "Lighten up, plenty of air, but more softly." I also have them echo the following phrases. Spoken in the middle voice, "May I please have a glass of milk." Spoken high and lightly, "I'd really like a glass of champagne," and spoken low and in chest voice, "Give me a (root) beer!" Now, when I need them to lighten at B above middle C and higher (B below middle C for baritone/basses), I merely ask for more of their champagne voice. An alternative to this is encouraging the "Mrs. Doubtfire" voice. This refers to Robin Williams in the movie of the same title, in which he speaks in head voice throughout. Show the film and have the students imitate the sound and feel the sensation. In addition, I also have them experiment with tone color front to back, by using a scale of one to ten. One is the darkest; ten the most nasal. We start at five on an AH vowel, darken to one and then brighten to ten. I then determine the best color for our next selection and say, "Give me a six." They now have a point of reference. This also works well when you want an increase in "apparent" dynamics. A higher number puts the sound more into the mask, makes the sound brighter and "apparently" louder.

Articulation: Diction and enunciation are last but not least. I really worked on this aspect last year and got tremendous adjudication scores in this area. I encourage my students to overemphasize as if they are speaking to someone who is hearing impaired or a friend across the room during a test! It's really just attention to detail, but you must reinforce it every moment by your own articulation, facial gestures, etc. If it's not right-do it again! In addition, I write the following palindrome on the board: "Sit on a potato pan Otis!" We enunciate this very clearly several times during our warm-up. When diction becomes muddled during a song, I only need to point to the phrase on the board to remedy the problem and regain the students' focus.

Additional resources:

Building Beautiful Voices. Paul Nesheim and Weston Noble. Roger Dean Publishing.

Choir Builders. Rollo Dilworth. Hal Leonard Corporation.

Experiencing Choral Music, Textbook Series. Emily Crocker and Audrey Snyder. McGraw Hill Glencoe.

Group Vocal Technique, VHS. Frauke Haaseman and James M. Jordan. Hinshaw Music Inc.

Ready, Set, Sing! VHS/DVD. Jeff Johnson. Santa Barbara Music Publishing, Inc.

Teaching Kids to Sing. Ken Phillips. Prentice Hall.

14

Q. My choir can't afford uniforms. What can I do?

A. I am a strong believer that the audience often hears with their eyes. I teach my students to look like a professional from the time that they enter the building, and particularly when they mount the risers. I have a definite location for each singer using the spacing method discussed earlier (Question 4). Early in each semester, I send a letter home indicating that black pants and shoes are the students' responsibility. I also tell every student that if this is a problem, please see me. I keep a closet full of black pants if needed. *White shirts and colorful ties are not a bad start,* however a ten dollar matching golf style shirt is a pretty easy and classy way to go. I spent about thirty-five dollars per student for matching vests and bowties, which really upgrades the look. It also tends to reinforce the special nature of choir and encourages the decorum befitting the classical music that we would perform as part of our concert. Students find it easier to sing "behind a costume" if you will. Organizations such as PTA, Site-Council, or *local service organizations such as Kiwanis or Lions will often provide funding* for this type of venture as well.

A true story: One of the most memorable administrator tales that I have to tell is when I was trying to build our local middle school choir and suddenly jumped from seventeen students to about forty. I went to my principal and told him of my dilemma and he responded with the nicest words I have ever heard, "You get the students and I'll get the uniforms." He made good on his promise and the ensemble rose to the challenge. They immediately performed at a higher level. I had asked them to be young adults and they even took on a more mature sound. It is perhaps the best investment that you can make for your ensemble.

15

Q. We sing only in English. I know that educationally we should sing in foreign languages. Where do I start?

A. When I began teaching, I was somewhat afraid of foreign languages. I had not taken foreign languages in high school, and eked my way through college German. I'm not even sure that we sang many other languages in my college choir so, as you can imagine, I was not well prepared. I knew, however, that as my groups improved, it was critical to move in this direction, *so one of my first pieces was "Praise Ye The Lord of Hosts" by Saint-Saens, which included both English and Latin texts.* I did my research consulting any pronunciation guides I could find, recordings, and a local priest, just for good measure! Low and behold, not only did the students do a great job, but they insisted on performing it in Latin, not English. To them it was part of what made choir special. It's what set them apart from those students not in choir. In addition, the blend immediately improved because of the pure vowels in the Latin text.

Since that time I've written several pieces that use parts of the mass as their text. "Sanctus," for instance, only uses that one Latin word, and the remainder is in English. This type of piece (of which there are many), is a great jumping-off selection. I've learned that most of us are reluctant to teach a foreign language because we are afraid of not getting it exactly right. "What will my colleagues say?" "What will the adjudicator think?" My answer is-it doesn't matter! *Dive in, do a little research, seek out recordings, or ask someone who speaks the language and go for it.* Sure, you won't get it perfect the first time, but each time it will get a little better, you'll become more comfortable, and your students will greatly profit from the opportunity.

A true story: One of the interesting things about being a published composer is that everyone immediately expects you to be an expert in all areas of choral music. Needless to say, when I was first published at the age of twenty-seven I was hardly an expert at anything! Soon the offers to conduct honor choirs came in and I felt compelled to accept. I also felt the need to perform selections in foreign languages. I recall programming Mozart's "Ave Verum Corpus" early on and wanting an accurate translation to share with the students. In our small town we have only one priest and although I was not Catholic, I had performed for weddings and knew Father Miles rather well. I went to his small parsonage with the printed music in hand and he sat down with me and slowly went about a literal translation of the text. I still have that copy with his pencil markings, and keep it as a reminder of the importance of doing your homework and research before performing any selection.

Additional resources:

Choral Singing in German, DVD. Darwin Sanders. Hal Leonard Corporation.

Choral Singing in Latin, DVD. Darwin Sanders. Hal Leonard Corporation.

Teaching Choral Literature with Foreign Language Texts. Carolyn Welch from Choral Music In the Junior High/Middle School, April 2007 Choral Journal. Janeal Krehbiel, editor janealk@sunflower.com

Translations and Annotations of Choral Repertoire, Vol. 1, Latin. Ron Jeffers. Earthsongs.

Translations and Annotations of Choral Repertoire, Vol. 2, German. Ron Jeffers. Earthsongs.

16

Q. I always have to talk over chattering in my choir. How do I get them to listen?

A. I'm convinced that some directors just seem to have a natural demeanor that helps them keep control over large groups of students. I have been somewhat blessed with this trait, but I also use some techniques that seem to work. I always begin the year, by telling the truth to my singers. I am here because I love music and I want to share it with them. I have three general rules.

1. Sing or Listen. *These are the only two options.* I will, however, allow you to chat for a minute or two between songs.

2. *Allow no gaps in the flow of the rehearsal.* We are constantly doing something. Either practicing a part, while the others sing theirs softly, or they are waiting to join, in tempo, the part we are going over with the other section, or we are singing together. I do as much as I can to not stop the choir from singing, but rather show through body language what I want from them vocally. This non-stop method requires you to know what you want to accomplish, and can be quite fatiguing, however, it allows little time for chatting. Again, spacing the ensemble as discussed earlier, engaging them in the music (sight-singing), and the mutual trust and respect that we have developed seldom results in much talking. I will, on occasion move a "chatterer" down right in front of me for a day, and if it is chronic, speak with them after class. My ensembles are special places in which the students want to remain, and therefore I have little problem with this.

3. I understand that choir is a social place. Therefore, after every fifteen to twenty minutes of rehearsal I *allow them a minute to chat with their neighbor*. When I stand before them again, the focus must return to me and the music. This builds mutual respect for one another. Sometimes I will use the age old "5-4-3-2-1" countdown to help regain attention as well.

17

Q. I have so many students in my choir I don't have time to take roll. Is there an easier way?

A. I like to *use numbered music, folders and racks*. This system is quick and easy. Generally I have very few absences and I make a point of knowing each student's name and location in the choir. Each student should have their own music and numbered folder, and be given a numbered slot for storage. Sharing music does not work well and encourages talking. Since subjective grading is difficult to do in a performance class, care of music can be an easy criteria. In addition, roll is easy to take by merely checking the folders that remain in the rack once class begins or towards the end of the rehearsal. If your choir utilizes uniforms, have the number of the uniform also coordinate with the folder.

18

Q. I don't have a budget for an accompanist and have to play the accompaniments myself. How can I get out from behind the piano?

A. Nothing improves the quality of a choir more than having a competent accompanist. There-I said it! Much the same as with budgeting for music purchases, educating your administrator is an important aspect of obtaining adequate funding for an accompanist. Most teacher contracts have a maximum number of students dictated for their classroom teachers. If you exceed this number, perhaps you are eligible for a teacher's aide. This hourly rate may not be enough to hire an accompanist, but can help in the process.

Seek out a volunteer. Often times with a little publicity, you can find someone in the community who would be happy to help. After all, most middle-school level literature is not terribly demanding.

Record your accompaniments. Most digital pianos have a sequencing feature that will allow you or an accompanist to record the part. You can also use a notation program such as Finale® to input the part and then play it back via the computer's speakers.

Sing a cappella. If you really want a challenge that is very beneficial for your students, have them practice a cappella, and then bring in an accompanist for the last few rehearsals and performance. It forces them to listen and be independent singers. I believe that it is next to impossible to retain decorum and actually hear what the choir is doing if you are playing or singing along. Make having an accompanist a priority.

Q. My choir does not sing with much facial expression. What can I do?

A. As a conductor, I was always animated and reflected the style of the music in my body language. That helps, but often is not enough. I find teenagers VERY passionate about things in their life, and I find that if we choose lyrics that are relevant, and discuss how the lyric relates to their own lives, expression will come somewhat naturally.

Another activity you can do is to *videotape the choir* and let them watch. They may think they are being expressive when in fact their look is rather deadpan. It is a good idea to *show them a DVD of fine ensembles* like the Indianapolis Children's Choir, under the direction of Henry Leck. They are very animated, and it is my understanding that he actually teaches the facial expression much like choreography. However, the natural exuberance of students engaged with music that they like is very enjoyable as well.

Use kinesthetics as part of your rehearsal. Jeff Johnson's video, Ready, Set, Sing includes some great ideas for incorporating face, hand and body motions into the choral warm-up and rehearsal. It will be difficult to sing in a deadpan manner when the music is learned in this fashion.

What they see is what you get. Rod Eichenberger does a great workshop on this topic which has been recorded on video.

Additional resources:

Ready, Set, Sing! VHS/DVD. Jeff Johnson. Santa Barbara Music Publishing, Inc.

What They See Is What You Get, VHS. Rodney Eichenberger. Santa Barbara Music Publishing, Inc.

20

Q. Sometimes my choir learns a piece easily and sounds great, and at other times it takes forever and they never sound good on the selection. Can you help?

A. Honestly, some chorals just sing better than others. It has to do with the *quality of the original song*. Does the tune stand alone without the harmonization? Does the key put the bulk of the notes in a *comfortable range*? Are there *varying textures*, i.e., unisons, two-part, call and answer, and fully harmonized sections? Have you sung through each line to see if the voice leading is natural? Is the text appropriate for young singers? Generally, ensembles sound better on pieces that are not unusually rangy, and on easy foreign languages such as Latin, which contains pure vowels with no diphthongs (double vowels such as long a and long i). Use arrangers and editors whose work you trust and remember, just because the piece is new doesn't mean that it is better than a tried and true selection that is in a similar style.

A true story: Once during a Q&A session a teacher asked me what my *least* favorite arrangement was. Quite frankly, it was an easy answer because there were several pieces I had arranged in my early days as a favor to my first publisher. I remarked that the piece was "Slow Down I'll Find You" from a Susan Anton movie. I went on to say that it had, "slowed down so much that no one found it" because it was not a great seller. To my chagrin, another teacher wildly waved her hand in the air. When I acknowledged her she said, "That song was my kids' favorite!" It just goes to show you that any given piece can be effective in the right situation.

Q. Choosing music has never really been a big deal for me. Is there a problem with just ordering music off of a recorded sampler?

A. *The music IS your curriculum.* Choose it wisely and carefully. Not only should it give your students a wide variety of choral experiences (from Renaissance to Rock!), but it should also be somewhat sequential in that as the year or years progress, the music becomes more demanding in range, flexibility and content.

Music samplers are great ways to hear a lot of new material, but make sure that you include live reading sessions and tried and true sessions as well. Seeing *what each line in the music does is essential* to the success of the piece with students. Professionals can sing anything, and *recordings can make almost any piece sound good.*

The music must meet several criteria. Is it a quality song? Do I like it? Do my students like it? Will my audience like it? Does it fit into a logical educational sequence of choral skill development? Does it expand my choir's awareness of the breadth and scope of choral music? Look for opportunities for all students to sing melody, harmony, counter-point, and to extend their range and flexibility as a singer.

A true story: Believe it or not, I never attended a reading session until I was published. Here on the West Coast my local retailer never offered sessions of this type. I would always go to their store, pick interesting titles from the browser boxes and return home to go through them with my accompanist. I do recall my first session however. It was sponsored by Stanton's Sheet Music in Columbus, Ohio. Now don't get me wrong, the Stanton's staff is very careful about their music selection, but quite frankly on that day only one piece out of sixty-five stood out! I realized at that point that I was very picky when it came to music choices. I still am! If you watch me at a reading session, a few times during the day I will quietly slip a single copy into my briefcase. In case you are wondering what the selection was on that day in Columbus, it was Dale Wood's "Slow Me Down, Lord."

The first reading session that I ever conducted was for a small music dealer in Huntington, West Virginia. Pied Piper Music hosted about fifty teachers from the surrounding area and what makes this day memorable had nothing to do with the music, but rather with lunch! I had recently completed a CPR class that was required of all teachers at my school and along with the class was basic instruction in the Heimlich maneuver to rescue a choking victim. Wouldn't you know that during the buffet lunch, one of the teachers began choking and I went around behind his chair and gave three upward thrusts of the diaphragm and out popped a sandwich. I now consider myself the "all-purpose" clinician. Funny thing is that three months later in a California restaurant I performed the Heimlich again, but thankfully have never had to do it since, and that was thirty years ago!

Q. How important is sight-singing? My students have great ears and seem to pick up the parts quickly, so do I really need to spend time on notation? What are the most important elements in sight-singing?

A. I firmly believe that we must make an effort to instruct students in total musicianship, including sight-singing. Since singing has always been an improvisational, aural experience, we tend to jump right in and teach them parts by rote instead of empowering our singers by teaching them to learn to read from the page. The entire dynamic of the rehearsal changes when students become engaged in the music. There are fewer discipline problems and greater focus as a result, not to mention the quicker absorption of the parts, which leaves the director the time and energy necessary to teach the choral art instead of pounding out parts. Here are my suggestions using an easy to remember acronym, RICE.

Rhythm: If you can *teach whole notes, half notes, quarter notes and basic eighth note rhythms*, you will have most of the necessary rhythmic skills needed for most pieces of music. You can use any method you wish; tap, clap, or chant various rhythmic figures of your choosing from a variety of sources. Just make sure that you do it at each rehearsal.

Intervals: *Teach your students to identify the most common intervals*, i.e., major 3rd, minor 3rd, perfect 4th, perfect 5th, major 6th, octave, down a minor 3rd and a perfect 4th with these examples or others of your choosing.

Major 3rd: Michael Row the Boat Ashore
Minor 3rd: Set Down Servant
Perfect 4th: Here Comes the Bride
Perfect 5th: Star Wars Theme
Major 6th: My Bonnie Lies Over the Ocean
Octave: Somewhere Over the Rainbow
Down a minor 3rd: Volga Boatman
Perfect 4th: Eine Kleine Nachtmusik

Point out these intervals whenever they occur in the music. Students will readily apply them. In addition, you may want to challenge your students to bring in contemporary songs which exemplify a given interval. For instance, the chorus of "Get the Party Started" by Pink begins with a minor 3rd, "I'm come." Also, make sure instrumentalists in your choir make the connection between reading notes on their instrument and singing those notes on their vocal instrument.

Connect the notes: *Teach students to connect the notes*. This is very easy to do. Just have your singers move by steps (within the scale) between the notes. Make a conscious effort to point out places in the music that move by step, and when singing an interval, confirm the size of the interval by singing the missing notes in between by step.

Eyes: Teach your students to use their eyes to identify notes and pitches they have sung in previous measures. I call this tonal memory. If they can remember what it sounded like elsewhere, the same note will sound the same here. This is also true of getting your pitch from another part that has recently sung the same pitch.

Sometimes the idea of teaching sight-singing is overwhelming, but remember that ninety percent of the skills a singer needs are illustrated above. You can continue to teach difficult rhythmic or harmonic passages by rote if necessary. Rote teaching will be a small percentage of what you do if the students can do the rest. Not all of your students will "get" sight-singing, but just imagine if half of them do. You will have more section leaders than you know what to do with and the rest will follow. Good luck and don't forget to give your students RICE every day!

A true story: I am embarrassed to say that I didn't do much teaching of sight-singing during my first several years of teaching, but when I went back for my second tenure, I taught basic intervals as part of the warm-up. Not surprisingly, after a few months the ensemble could make music the first time through a piece, and I vividly remember one of my baritones looking up at me and saying, "Now I get it." We have many instrumentalists who read, but only need to be shown the correlation between playing an instrument and sight-singing. Also, let's put to rest the age old adage, "we have the musicians and the singers." Music literacy is important to everyone.

Additional resources:

The Choral Approach to Sight Singing. Joyce Eilers and Emily Crocker. Hal Leonard Corporation.

Patterns of Sound. Joyce Eilers and Emily Crocker. Hal Leonard Corporation.

Sing on Sight. Audrey Snyder. Hal Leonard Corporation.

23

Q. I want to do some choreography with my choir, but when they start moving they stop singing. Can they do both?

A. The short answer is yes! However there are several criteria that must be met in order to do both effectively.

Learn the song well first. As a choral director, this is my first priority. It is very difficult to go back and fix elements of the piece once we start moving.

Use moves that match the music. Literal choreography will actually reinforce the learning of lyrics and can enhance the ebb and flow of the phrase.

Use primarily upper body movement except during intros, interludes and dance breaks. We don't even ask professionals to do a lot of dancing while singing unless they are supported by recorded vocal tracks.

Use part of the choir only. Some students will be uncomfortable moving and others are born to dance. If the group is large enough, you can have part of them "grooving" in the background or on risers, while the dancers do their thing down in front.

A true story: Movement and music-what a concept! I remember quite vividly when I realized that to just stand and sing was not the most effective way to perform popular music. It was about twenty years ago when I was conducting a reading session in Southern California, representing the Jenson catalog along with two new acquaintances, Mac Huff and John Jacobson, representing the Hal Leonard catalog. I did my usual presentation of merely conducting the piece, while John and Mac really "sold" their pieces by not only reading them, but then staging and simply choreographing them as well. I said to myself, "That's the way to sell choral music." I know it may sound rather crass, but realize that as a conductor of popular music, you are selling the piece to your audience. In this day and age of visual stimulation, popular music is missing something without staging. Now the challenge is to do it effectively without losing the vocal essence. Good luck!

Additional resources:

John Jacobson's Riser Choreography, DVD. John Jacobson. Hal Leonard Corporation.

Kids Gotta Move!, DVD. John Jacobson. Hal Leonard Corporation.

Kids On Stage, VHS. John Jacobson. Hal Leonard Corporation.

24

Q. Students are always being pulled out of my class in order to do other more "academic" activities. It's very disconcerting. What can I do to lessen this tradition?

A. *Provide high standards in your classroom.* Support school-wide efforts in regards to attendance, application of state standards and "on task" class time. *Let other staff members see what you are doing* by providing daytime concerts for the student body and staff. Cite and tactfully post data and articles that support an increase in test scores and brain function by participation in the arts. The Elementary and Secondary Education Act (No Child Left Behind), declares the arts core education. Most states also include the arts in mandated curriculum. When applicable, include music that supports other curriculums, for example, selections which include lyrics by well known poets (tie-in with language arts), historical musicals like *The Adventures of Lewis & Clark, Dig It!* or *Go West!* (with social studies), or *Update: Earth* (science). Also, avoid pulling students out of other classes yourself. (Do unto others…) Lastly, *be a team player.* Participate in school-wide committees and social activities.

Educating your fellow staff members is a life-long pursuit. Understand that they reflect the general community in believing that music and other arts curriculum seem to fall into the category of entertainment, because that is what music means to them. Our job as educators is to help them understand that without art, we will have little to read and write about! In addition, music provides a sense of community that so many young people need today.

A true story: There is so much to learn when you are teaching, and the importance of building good relationships with fellow staff members is an important lesson. I remember quite vividly my "run-in" with Pat Redelsperger, the veteran social studies teacher at my first middle school. It was my first concert and I desperately needed at least one rehearsal on the combined band and choir selection, so without polling the staff I scheduled an extra rehearsal in the middle of the day. A few minutes into the rehearsal, Pat charged in and made no bones about the fact that I was not to pull students out of her class ever again! I was quite taken aback by this feisty sixty year old veteran teacher, but none the less learned that she was not just being obstinate, but rather cared as passionately about her subject as I did about mine. From that day forward we became close friends. I never pulled students from her classes again, and she never pulled them from mine!

Additional resources:

Dr. Tim Lautzenheiser, www.attitudeconcepts.com

No Subject Left Behind, A Guide to Arts Education Opportunities in the 2001 NCLB Act. (Google for various sources and information)

25

Q. My boys only want to sing low and yet the music calls for them to sing in the middle range or above. How can I get them to vocalize higher?

A. *Warm-up with familiar melodies in higher keys.* Do these by rote so that the student does not see how high the notes rest in the staff. *Exercise the head voice during warm-ups.* Do sighs and sirens. I do an exercise called "lasers" with the entire choir. It's a little hard to explain, but basically it borrows a simulated laser battle from the Star Wars movies. Students imitate dueling light saber sounds (bee-you) from falsetto to chest voice (about A above middle C to A below), followed by a chromatic scale downward between the two pitches.

Where a masculine lyric exists, have the young men *vocalize in unison with the women*, particularly if the melody lies in the lower chest voice for the women. (Earth, Wind and Fire songs do this all the time. It's called unison prime.) Most guys love competition, so don't forget to tell them, "The guy with the most notes wins!"

In addition, remember that young men associate singing high with femininity. It's not a bad idea to search out and play recordings of macho guys singing tenor and in falsetto.

A true story: Since leaving my second stint as a middle school choir director, I'm often asked by my successor Fred Wichmann to come in and work with the boys. It is fun to drop back in, particularly when the responsibility for the program is no longer on my shoulders. I am convinced that if possible, boys at this level should be taught separately from the girls and here is why. They will sing anything you ask when not around the females. In fact, when we are working on their part, and reach a section that is girls only, without thinking we all jump up the octave and sing out! They love it, and think nothing of the octave jump. Weird but true!

Additional resources:

The Boys Changing Voice, DVD. Henry Leck. Hal Leonard Corporation

Enhancing Musicality through Movement, VHS. Rodney Eichenberger. Santa Barbara Music Publishing, Inc.

Strategies for Teaching Junior High and Middle School Male Singers. Terry Barham. Santa Barbara Music Publishing, Inc.

Success for Adolescent Singers, DVD, Patrick K. Freer, Ed.D., Choral Excellence Inc.

26

Q. My sopranos sound very screechy when they sing high. What am I doing wrong?

A. *Warm the voice thoroughly before singing.* Chances are that they are pulling the chest voice up into the upper register. At about B above middle C they need to *roll into the head voice.* Also, how high is high? I warm my middle school females up to C above the staff, but rarely do we sing above about a G. Remember that hitting the note is not necessarily singing the note. *Lighten the voice in the upper part of the staff and above.* (See Question 3) Play examples (or even better, provide good high school singers as models) of a beautifully balanced female voice and encourage your singers to emulate the sound.

Additional resources:

Building Beautiful Voices. Paul Nesheim and Weston Noble. Roger Dean Publishing.

Choir Builders. Rollo Dilworth. Hal Leonard Corporation.

Daily Workout for a Beautiful Voice, VHS/DVD. Charlene Archibeque and Charlotte Adams. Santa Barbara Music Publishing, Inc.

Ready, Set, Sing! VHS/DVD. Jeff Johnson. Santa Barbara Music Publishing, Inc.

Teaching Kids to Sing. Ken Phillips. Prentice Hall

27

Q. My altos sound very edgy and raw when they sing below the staff. How can I help them sound rich and full?

A. One of the most important things to remember about upper elementary and middle school female singers is that *they are all (for the most part), mezzo sopranos.* Their voices have not really settled into classified soprano and alto ranges. Generally those who gravitate to the alto part are those who don't wish to sing high. Often directors tend to put students with good ears or those who have background on piano or an instrument on those parts. That being said; *watch the range of alto parts,* looking for parts that do not go below Bb below middle C. Also, *don't allow them to push* to try to sing loudly down in this register. Singing a bit softer will take a lot of the edginess off the sound.

Additional resources:

Building Beautiful Voices. Paul Nesheim and Weston Noble. Roger Dean Publishing.

Choir Builders. Rollo Dilworth. Hal Leonard Corporation.

Daily Workout for a Beautiful Voice, VHS/DVD. Charlene Archibeque and Charlotte Adams. Santa Barbara Music Publishing, Inc.

Ready, Set, Sing! VHS/DVD. Jeff Johnson. Santa Barbara Music Publishing, Inc.

Teaching Kids to Sing. Ken Phillips. Prentice Hall

28

Q. My boys match pitch pretty well, but have trouble staying on their part. They always want to sing the melody. What can I do?

A. The simple answer is to find choral arrangements that *give the melody to the young men.* (I make a concerted effort to do so, much to the chagrin of the sopranos who are not used to singing a harmony part). In most school programs, the *boys have just not had as much experience* singing as the girls have. Singing has often not been the cool thing to do, and they are coming into your program with little experience using their voice. Therefore, the melody, or repetitive melodic parts are the most effective. Also, look for ostinati that are in a comfortable range for the young men and that also compliment the melody. I like repetitive rhythmic motives for the guys. It also helps to find easy melodies that the guys can sing alone without the competition and distraction of other parts going on. *Find a simple unison or easy two-part piece or pieces that will feature them.*

Additional resources:

The Boys Changing Voice, DVD. Henry Leck. Hal Leonard Corporation.

Enhancing Musicality through Movement, VHS. Rodney Eichenberger. Santa Barbara Music Publishing, Inc.

Strategies for Teaching Junior High and Middle School Male Singers. Terry Barham. Santa Barbara Music Publishing, Inc.

Q. I have a non-select choir that does a pretty good job, but I know that a third of them could really be great. Should I start auditioning and limiting those who can be in the program?

A. In public education *it is essential to offer a choir that all students with the desire to sing may attend.* Remember, perfection is not (in my opinion) the ultimate goal. Fostering the joy of music is. That does not mean that you should put up with weak effort, or a poor performance. I have found that non-select ensembles can reach a high level of performance on moderately easy literature. Save the art songs and more esoteric pieces for your select ensembles. These groups could *meet after school, lunch or other periods. Many students just want to be part of the community of singers.* We provide the closest thing to a family that many of them may ever have.

A true story: I believe it was my fourth year of teaching when it struck me; I should not be teaching music for its own sake, but rather for the goal of fostering individual growth *through* music. I was known as "firm but fair" by students and colleagues, but my goal had been musical perfection. I was, after all, a perfectionist. I expected it of myself and my students. In the process I would become frustrated and take that frustration out on my students. Hardly a day would go by without at least one of my students crying, and one day it became clear to me that music was not the end all and be all, but rather, the vehicle. From that day forward I put students before the music, even if it meant that my groups would not be as polished. Interestingly enough, when I changed my thinking and the way I addressed my ensembles (with joy and laughter instead of intimidation) they started to perform at an even higher level. Remember that music can be performed perfectly and yet if no one (performer or audience) is moved, in my opinion no real music is made.

Additional resources:

A Place in the Choir. John Jacobson. Hal Leonard Corporation.

Best Friends, Worst Enemies. Michael Thompson. Ballentine Books.

Up Front! Becoming the Complete Choral Director. Guy B. Webb. E. C. Schirmer Music Company.

Q. My principal insists that everyone sing in the choir. About a third of them don't want to be there. It's a nightmare. What can I do?

A. This is a real predicament. My only prerequisite is that *the student must want to be there. Make every effort to educate your administrator* about the difference between a performance class like choir and academic classes like general music, guitar, music appreciation. In those classes, the performance of one individual does not generally affect another; choir, on the other hand, does. Draw comparisons with competitive sports teams on which students who do not have the desire must play. *Suggest alternatives* to music performance such as student aide, working on music software at the computer, playing percussion or running the sound system. Some students are just not comfortable performing. Suggest that only those who want to perform in public will have to, but everyone needs to participate in rehearsal. Then keep it moving so that there is little time to disagree.

Additional resources:

Best Friends, Worst Enemies. Michael Thompson. Ballentine Books.

The Pressured Child. Michael Thompson. Ballentine Books.

Raising Cain, Protecting the Emotional Life of Boys. Dan Kindlon and Michael Thompson. Ballentine Books.

31

Q. My singers always seem to go flat in pitch. What's the solution?

A. I have found that generally singers bring their speaking skills into the choir rehearsal. That includes unprepared air, horizontal resonators, unarticulated consonants etc. *Lack of adequate air is perhaps the most obvious reason* for pitch sag. Hissing breathing exercises and learning the sensation of a full breath are essential to quality singing. Also, when students pull the chest voice up above B there is a tendency to go flat. *Get them out of the chest voice and into the head voice.* Finally, emphasize pure vowels where possible, and *tall vertical singing*. Drop the jaw and raise the soft palate as if you had a hot potato in the back of your throat. Sometimes lifting the eyebrows will accomplish this as well. (See questions 3 and 13.)

Additional resources:

Building Beautiful Voices. Paul Nesheim and Weston Noble. Roger Dean Publishing.

Choir Builders. Rollo Dilworth. Hal Leonard Corporation.

Daily Workout for a Beautiful Voice, VHS/DVD. Charlene Archibeque and Charlotte Adams. Santa Barbara Music Publishing, Inc.

Ready, Set, Sing! VHS/DVD. Jeff Johnson. Santa Barbara Music Publishing, Inc.

Teaching Kids to Sing. Ken Phillips. Prentice Hall

32

Q. The vocal lines that we sing sound "mushy" and lack energy. What am I doing wrong?

A. *Uniform vowel shape creates a beautiful and warm sound, while energy is derived from careful attention to consonants.* Remember to emphasize beginning, internal and final consonants. Every great choir that I have heard tenderly caresses each consonant in a uniform way—it is very exciting.

Direct students to *underline the most important words of each phrase* and then slightly emphasize those words when singing. Sometimes it is a bit challenging to determine which words are the most important, but it will not be words such as an, but, or the.

The phrase should rise and fall. When singing, *have the students slightly race up the phrase and slightly slow down the back side.*

Try the following exercises. Write this phrase on the board: "Sit on a potato pan Otis." (Backward it is the same, a palindrome.) Practice it during warm-up, and then point to it, mid-song, when students start to forget the importance of enunciation. Also during warm-ups you may sing this exercise: "Many mumbling mice are making merry music in the moonlight. Mighty nice."

A true story: What teacher doesn't look forward to a visit from a returning student? Stacie had moved to Reno, Nevada at the beginning of the year, but came back for a visit right before Christmas vacation. We had been working hard on vowel uniformity in order to achieve blend, but had spent little time on consonants, so the vitality was missing. Wouldn't you know that Stacie brought back the solution from her new teacher in Reno: "Sit on a potato pan Otis" was shared and applied. Thank you Stacie, and thank you to that anonymous teacher in Reno!

Additional resource:

Ready, Set, Sing! VHS/DVD. Jeff Johnson. Santa Barbara Music Publishing, Inc.

33

Q. A piece we have worked on is just not coming together and our concert is next week. What should I do?

A. The success of a performance is really up to you. I don't know how many concerts I have attended where the music is just too difficult. I would rather hear a unison piece performed musically than a thicker harmonization done poorly. *Never show them what you cannot do*. Students know when a selection is not ready for public performance. Do fewer pieces. No one ever complained about a program that was too short! An alternative is to *do only a portion* or movement of the piece, or perhaps save it for the next concert.

A true story: Several years ago I had the joy of hearing the Toronto Children's Chorus perform Bach's "Bist Du Bei Mir" in unison at an ACDA conference in San Diego. It was beautiful, moving and musical, and it reminded me that thickness of harmony in accompanied pieces is just not necessary. Tone, line, dynamics, and intonation are far more important than a big chord.

34

Q. Some of my singers learn more quickly than others. How do I keep them engaged and challenged in rehearsal particularly when another section or group is working more slowly, or even struggling?

A. Good question. This takes a little work, but about a third of your students will be on the fast track. You can make them mini section leaders by putting a slower student to the left and right of them. You don't have to make a big deal out of this, but usually slower students just need to hear the part sung correctly around them. In older ensembles you can actually assign section leaders and let them run section rehearsals. Many of the chorals published today include a CD with part specific tracks. Get three or four boom boxes and place them in the corners of the room. Put the "fast track" students in charge and run mini section rehearsals for five minutes or so. It really works. Ultimately, you will want to break out the high achievers into a small ensemble for perhaps a more challenging piece at the concert. Allow other students to challenge and be included in the ensemble as well.

35

Q. I'm a band teacher who now has to teach choir. Where do I begin?

A. About ten years ago several publishers decided to create *choral method books* that are similar to band method books. They teach basic skills in a sequential manner and provide graded literature as well. I have listed my favorites below. In addition, contact your local music dealer regarding *choral selections that have stood the test of time* and sell well year after year. There is a reason for this; they work and are generally well-liked by teachers, students and audiences. Apply my PASTA skills (Posture, Air, Shape, Tone and Articulation) described in question thirteen. Go to conferences and get recordings of quality ensembles at your students' level and *imitate* their sound. Also, sing more yourself in a community or church ensemble. Band directors can make great choir directors because of their attention to musicianship and accuracy.

Additional resources:

Essential Elements, Choral Method. Emily Crocker and John Leavitt. Hal Leonard Corporation.

Experiencing Choral Music, Textbook Series. McGraw Hill Glencoe.

Ready, Set, Sing! VHS/DVD. Jeff Johnson. Santa Barbara Music Publishing, Inc.

Teaching Kids to Sing. Ken Phillips. Prentice Hall.

Up Front! Becoming the Complete Choral Director. Guy B. Webb. E. C. Schirmer Music Company.

36

Q. I just graduated from college and feel that my choral methods class did not adequately prepare me for this! Where do I begin?

A. Don't feel badly. I felt the same way when I graduated with my bachelor's degree. Find a good choral method and use it. The reality is that there is a lot *of on the job training* that takes place during your first few years. *You will learn as you go.* I remember starting my 7th and 8th graders on SATB music, only to end up with SA mud! Finally I figured out what the boys were able to do and proceeded from there. My saving grace was my upbeat personality and God-given *musicianship*. Probably yours too!

Additional resources:

Experiencing Choral Music, Textbook Series. McGraw Hill Glencoe.

Ready, Set, Sing! VHS/DVD. Jeff Johnson. Santa Barbara Music Publishing, Inc.

Teaching Kids to Sing. Ken Phillips. Prentice Hall.

Up Front! Becoming the Complete Choral Director. Guy B. Webb. E. C. Schirmer Music Company.

Q. Some days I just don't feel like teaching. Can you help me get over the blues?

A. We have all been there! I have often said that teaching music is the hardest job you will ever love. Unless you have been there, few people realize the energy and dedication that it takes to be a music teacher. I do know, however, that we forge relationships with kids more than any other teacher in the school. *It is truly a higher calling.* It is also true that *YOU make the weather in the classroom.* If you are engaged and upbeat, the students will be the same. Perhaps you need to do *something different* this year. How about starting the year with a musical or perhaps having a winter concert in January that doesn't use the usual holiday selections? I've often asked the question, "How would you teach differently if you didn't have to put on a concert?" Most people respond, "I'd teach more sight-reading, improvisation, voice builders, and solos." It's interesting that all those things are called for in the national standards, but we get so busy preparing songs for the concert that we forget, or don't have time to do them.

A true story: Some years ago I was having a conversation with my good friend, John Jacobson. I was lamenting that I never got to write that "hit" song. He responded very simply, "you have a higher calling." It struck me as funny at the time, but now I know what he was talking about. There can be nothing more important than positively affecting the lives of students. We have that opportunity every day!

Additional resources:

Change Your Thoughts, Change Your Life: Living the Wisdom of the Tao. Wayne W. Dyer. Hay House.

Tuesdays with Morrie: an Old Man, a Young Man and Life's Greatest Lesson. Mitch Albom. Doubleday Books.

38

Q. I have a small clique of girls that seem to always be against me. It is very disruptive and disconcerting. How can I get control of the situation?

A. I always found that if you can treat the situation with humor, sometimes even ignoring it, the problem will go away. *Don't take the bait.* Since my rehearsals were always fast paced and focused, quite frankly, there wasn't much time to mess around. Without losing your temper, *just ask the offenders to meet with you after class.* Do not take out your frustration on all of the students. After all, most of them are doing exactly what you are asking of them. If a heart to heart discussion doesn't do the trick, *you may need to ask them to leave the ensemble.* I always tell them that we are still friends, but choir is a place where time and focus are really important. They are also welcome to come back if and when they are ready. Sometimes they will take others with them, but the net result is a positive one. Those students who are on task are often just waiting for you to fix the problem. As I always say, "no one is indispensable." One singer is a solo, two a duet, three a trio, etc. It is better to have those who really want to sing in the ensemble, and to remove those who are a constant distraction.

Additional resource:

Best Friends, Worst Enemies. Michael Thompson. Ballentine Books.

39

Q. Everyone wants to stand on the top row of risers. Is there an equitable way to determine who stands where?

A. Weston Noble has a unique tonal system for placing singers. We at the elementary and middle school level have little use for that technique because more often than not either height of the student or the ability of the singer to stay focused dictates back row position. I almost invariably would have the most hyperactive right in front of me, and *by default the most focused ended up on the top row*. My friend Travis Rogers uses a *challenge system* where a student can challenge for an upper row by singing a passage from a selected piece of music and challenging a student whose position he or she would like to occupy. This works well in upper Jr. high and high school, but I prefer *row rotation* for rehearsals. Each rehearsal a different row stands in front. This allows you to hear more of your students, and allows them to hear differently as well. In the end, it is your call and it may very well be "what makes the best looking picture" for the concert that prevails. Remember, the choir is not a democracy, it is a benevolent dictatorship!

40

Q. In my choir I have several students whose religious beliefs prevent them from singing some of our songs. What can I do to include them?

A. This is a sensitive subject, but I always made an effort not to make a big deal out of it. The *students were always excused at their discretion*, and I would *offer them alternative activities* such as the opportunity to turn pages, play percussion instruments, or merely sit and listen. On occasion I would suggest that they *sing a neutral vowel* such as "oo" instead of the lyrics that were in question. In the final analysis, the student is often torn between parental dictates and their own desire to be part of the group. With little fuss, include them in any way possible.

41

Q. My choir sings quite well, but I feel that we are at a plateau. Do you have any suggestions for improvement?

A. This is the third in a series of acronyms that outline important elements of choral technique. I would suggest that you start with PAS-TA (posture, air, shape, tone, articulation – see question 13) and RICE (rhythm, intervals, connection, eyes – see question 22), before moving ahead to this series of techniques or SPEED.

Stress: *Word Stress or emphasis.* Have your students take a good look at each phrase, perhaps underlining the most important word or words. Then have them sing the line, placing a bit of emphasis upon the high-lighted words. This will greatly add to the meaning and expressive-ness of the text. Make sure that you have spent time determining which words are most important before giving your singers the opportunity for input.

Phrasing: *Emphasize phrasing.* Students should learn that a musical phrase has a rise and fall like a spoken sentence. If desired, you can have them "rush up" the first half of the phrase and "slow down" the back half. Or, slightly crescendo up and diminuendo down. Have the singers make an arc with the hand and arm as they move through the phrase.

Energy: *Energize the performance.* Singing is a very energetic experi-ence. It must involve providing vitality to the line, much as you would whisper intently. Emphasizing consonants will also add vitality to the line. Have students put their weight on the ball of the foot and lean forward for intensity. On soft passages, have them "shout inside." Your animated facial expressions will often energize singers as well. Get your head out of the music and make eye contact with your students (their eyes should constantly be on you as well). Give melismas such as Glo-ria from "Angels We Have Heard on High" definition by having a third of the singers place an "n" before each "oh" in Gloria. (Thanks to Wil-liam Denning!)

Expressiveness: *Internalize the text for increased expressiveness.* Often it is good to discuss the meaning of the text prior to singing a note of the song. Have the students recite the lines as a poem. Relate the text to the feelings that a young person might have about a given text i.e., "away, I'm bound away, cross the wide Missouri" might conjure up feelings of leaving someone they love behind.

Dynamic Contrast: *Apply more dynamic contrast.* This is simple but often overlooked. Choirs usually begin a piece too loudly. Make sure that there is some place to go dynamically in the piece. Choruses are usually louder and more intense than verses. Often bridges are more legato or flowing. If there is a repeated phrase, it should either grow each time it is sung or diminish. Long sounds, for example half notes or longer, should not just sit there. Crescendo, decrescendo, or give each long note some rise and fall like a mini-phrase. If you get to the last chorus and it needs more volume, try having the singers brighten the sound by bringing it forward in the mask instead of singing louder to the point of tone deterioration.

These are just a few ideas to improve your choral performance. What I have found is that we get so busy teaching notes these obvious points are overlooked. Emphasizing SPEED will help to convey the meaning of the song. At times these elements are more important than choral skill. Who hasn't been moved by a group of singers that really gets into it, even at the expense of the choral sound? Ideally, we can and should do both.

Additional resources:

Creating Artistry through Movement in the Choral Rehearsal, DVD. Henry Leck. Hal Leonard Corporation.

Ready, Set, Sing! VHS/DVD. Jeff Johnson. Santa Barbara Music Publishing, Inc.

Q. What are some of your favorite warm-ups and voice builders?

A. When dealing with middle school singers, I like to adapt familiar warm-ups and place them in the key of F. This really helps the boy altos and changing voices, because middle C can be too high after a few stepwise progressions, and the octave lower is too low to start. Try

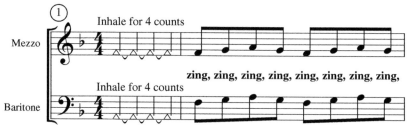

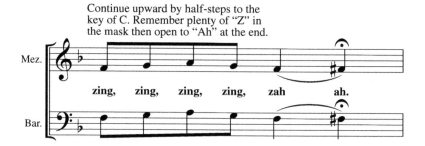

these!

Continue upward an octave to F. You want short, diaphramatic bursts, fully open "Ah." Think hot potato in mouth!

Shape each vowel in a vertical fashion

Full breath here!

DON'T FORGET 4 COUNTS OF AIR!

Continue upward by half-steps to E♭ or F. Remember to encourage a softer, lighter, "champagne" head voice from B to F.

You really can't continue this exercise upward, but you can start it lower as boys' voices mature, eventually starting on C or B♭

SiNG 6-7-8!

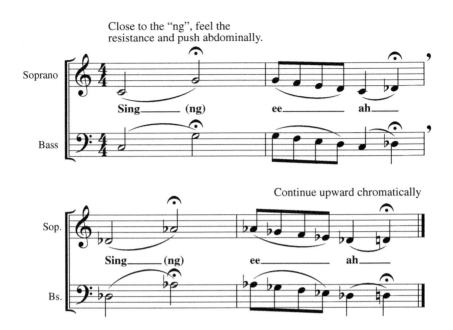

Additional resources:

Building Beautiful Voices. Paul Nesheim and Weston Noble. Roger Dean Publishing.

Choir Builders. Rollo Dilworth. Hal Leonard Corporation.

Daily Workout for a Beautiful Voice, VHS/DVD. Charlene Archibeque and Charlotte Adams. Santa Barbara Music Publishing, Inc.

Ready, Set, Sing! VHS/DVD. Jeff Johnson. Santa Barbara Music Publishing, Inc.

Teaching Kids to Sing. Ken Phillips. Prentice Hall

43

Q. I've been teaching at the high school level for several years, and now I'm going to be conducting a middle school choir. Do you have a list of "tried and true" materials that can get me started?

A. The middle school or Jr. high level is perhaps the most challenging in that, depending upon size and scheduling, your choice of music and voicing will vary. You should continue to insist on basic choral technique (PASTA–Question 13), and a sight-singing choral method. If you are fortunate enough to be able to teach separate treble and tenor/bass choirs this is ideal, but requires extensive 2part/SSA and TB/TTB/TBB materials, carefully chosen for both their ability level and their intellectual level. My experience has been with mixed ensembles at this level, and the list below reflects this.

3-part mixed chorus

African Noel	3pt.	Johnson	Heritage
Ave Verum	3pt	Mozart/Eilers	Hal Leonard
Blue Skies	3pt	Berlin/Emerson	Hal Leonard
Boatman Stomp	SAB	Grey	Schirmer
Cantate Domino	3pt	Poorman	BriLee
Carol of the Bells	3pt	Leontovich/Wilhousky	Fisher
Didn't My Lord Deliver...	3pt	Emerson	Hal Leonard
Dust in the Wind	3pt	arr. Emerson	Hal Leonard
Gloria	SAB	Vivaldi/Robinson	Warner
Good Timber Grows	3pt/SATB	Emerson	Hal Leonard
Hallelujah Amen	SAB	Handel/Vance	Schirmer
Hey, for the Dancing!	SAB	Bardos/Connor/Walker	Shawnee
Hosanna in Excelsis	SAB	Di Lasso/Snyder	Warner
Jubilate Deo	3pt	Crocker	Hal Leonard
Les Miserables Medley	3pt	arr. Emerson	Hal Leonard
Let Me Ride	3pt	Emerson	Hal Leonard
Memory	3pt	Webber/Huff	Hal Leonard

Pie Jesu	3pt	Lightfoot	Heritage
Praise Ye the Lord of Hosts	3pt	Saint-Saens/Eilers	Hal Leonard
The Rhythm of Life	SAB	Coleman/Fields/Leavitt	Studio PR
Sanctus	3pt	Emerson	Hal Leonard
Scarborough Fair	3pt	Emerson	Hal Leonard
Set Down Servant	3pt	Emerson	Hal Leonard
Shenandoah	SAB	Althouse	Alfred
Shine On Me	SAB	Dilworth	Hal Leonard
Shoshone Love Song	3pt	Emerson	Hal Leonard
Sing For Joy	SAB	Purcell/Hopson	Jenson
Sweet Singing in the Choir	3pt	Crocker	Hal Leonard
This Little Light of Mine	3pt	Johnson	Jenson
The Tiger	3pt	Porterfield	Heritage
Til The Stars Fall From…	SAB	Albrecht/Althouse	Alfred
Time Gone	3pt	Emerson	Hal Leonard
The Turtle Dove	3pt	Spevacek	Hal Leonard
Where Do the Stars Go	3pt	Porterfield	Heritage
Where E're You Walk	3pt	Handel/Emerson	Hal Leonard
White Christmas	3pt	Berlin/Bacak	Hal Leonard
Winter Wonderland	3pt	Smith/Bernard/Bacak	Warner
With Songs of Rejoicing	S/B	Hopson	Fischer

SSA

Al Shlosha D'varim	SA	Naplan	Boosey
Alleluja	SSA	Mozart/Spevacek	Hal Leonard
Angels Divine	SSA	Berg/Leck	Hal Leonard
Annie Laurie	U/2pt	Rentz	BriLee
Didn't My Lord Deliver...	SSA	Berg/Leck	Hal Leonard
Glorificamus Te	SSA	Butler	Hal Leonard
I'm Going to Sing	3pt. treble	Berg/Leck	Hal Leonard
Praise Ye the Lord of Hosts	SSA	Saint-Saens/Eilers	Hal Leonard
Simple Gifts	SSA	Coates	Shawnee
Sing Alleluia, Sing	SSA	Knowles	Jenson

TTB

3 Contemporary Latin Settings	TTB	Estes	Shawnee
Boatman Stomp	3-pt.	Gray	G. Schirmer
Born, Born in Bethlehem	TTB	Moore	BriLee
Bound for Jubilee	TTBB	Eilers	Studio PR
Bring Him Home	TTBB	Leavitt	Hal Leonard
The Chariot Spiritual	TTB	Moore	Brilee
Child of God	TTB	Crocker	Hal Leonard
He Ain't Heavy....	TTBB	Arr. Althouse	Alfred
If You've Only Got a Moustache	TB	Cooper	Somerset
Lo, How a Rose...	TTBB	Praetorius	G. Schirmer
Madrigals for Tenor/Bass	TTB	Arr. Porterfield	Hal Leonard
Poison Ivy	TBB	Arr. Shaw	Hal Leonard
Sing Hodie Noel!	TTB	Wagner	SMP
Sing Me a Song of a Lad...	TB	Leavitt	Hal Leonard
Streets of London	TB	Lewis	TRO
Two Renaissance Chorals for Men	TBB	Arr. Robinson	Belwin
When I Was Single	TB	Hardwick	Ditson

44

Q. I have a very advanced ensemble that includes 9th graders. We can perform moderate SATB literature. What are your suggestions?

A. You are indeed fortunate to have an ensemble with such ability. Below is a list of some of my favorite SATB selections, some are for more mature ensembles, but all are quality selections.

All SATB unless noted

A Savior from on High	Paulus	AMSI
Agnus Dei	Hassler/Leavitt	Hal Leonard
Ain't That Good News (Folio)	Hogan/Purifoy	Hal Leonard
And So It Goes	Joel/Shaw	Hal Leonard
Angels' Carol	Rutter	Hinshaw
Ave Maria	Helvering	Hal Leonard
Ave Maria	Biebl	Hinshaw
Ave Verum Corpus	Mozart	Schirmer
Bile Them Cabbage Down	Wilberg	Hinshaw
Blow, Blow Thou Winter Wind	Rutter	Oxford
Bridge Over Troubled Water	Simon/Shaw	Shawnee
Bring a Torch Jeannette, Isabella	Andrews	Shawnee Press
Cloudburst	Whitacre	Walton
Daniel, Daniel, Servant of the Lord	Moore	Warner
Dirait-on	Lauridsen	Peer Music
Do a Little Somethin'	Fry	Kimmel
Dry Your Tears, Afrika	Williams/Snyder	Hal Leonard
Festival Sanctus	Leavitt	Warner
Glory of the Father	Hovland	Walton
Grace	Hayes	Beckenhorst

Hear My Prayer	Hogan	Hal Leonard
I Have Longed for Thy Saving Health	Byrd/Whitehead	H.W. Gray
I'll Be Seeing You	Arr. Mattson	Hal Leonard
I'm a Train	Knight	Hal Leonard
I'm Gonna Sing Til the Spirit...	Hogan	Hal Leonard
If I Can't Love Her	arr. Emerson	Hal Leonard
In My Life	Arr. Emerson	Hal Leonard
Jamaican Market Place	Farrow	Gentry
Jazz Gloria	Sleeth	Hinshaw
Joyful, Joyful	Beethoven/Warren/Emerson	Hal Leonard
Kyrie Eleison	Kean	Pavane
Kyrie Eleison	McClure	Earthsongs
The Last Words of David	Thompson	E.C. Schirmer
Little Lamb	Phillips	G. Schirmer
The Little Road to Bethlehem	Rose/Head	Boosey & Hawkes
Lullaby	Joel/Huff	Hal Leonard
Mary, Did You Know?	Arr. Bock	Fred Bock Music
Movin' On	Hannisian	Shawnee Press
Nations Shall Learn War No More	Richards	Lawson-Gould
Neighbors' Chorus	Offenbach	Broude Brothers
O Sifuni Mungu	Maddux/McCall/Emerson	Hal Leonard
Pie Jesu	Webber/Leavitt	Hal Leonard
Praise the Lord	Handel/Hopson	Flammer
Rejoice and Sing Out His Praises	Hayes	Hinshaw
River in Judea	Markus/Leavitt	Warner
Seed to Sow	Smith/Emerson	Hal Leonard
Shepherd Me, Lord	Kingsley/Knight	Bourne
Sit Down Servant	Twine	Hinshaw
Somewhere	Edgerton	Hal Leonard
Their Hearts Were Full of Spring	Arr. Shaw	Hal Leonard
Three Hungarian Folk-Songs	Lloyd/Seiber	G. Schirmer

Three Madrigals	Diemer	Boosey & Hawkes
Ubi caritas	Durufle	Durand S.A (Hal Leonard)
Wailie, Wailie (Water is Wide)	DeCormier	G. Schirmer
When I Lay Me Down to Sleep	Mulholland	Colla Voce
Winter's on the Wing	Norman/Simon/Leavitt	Hal Leonard
You are the New Day	David/Knight	Hal Leonard

45

Q.
Do you have a list of your favorite chorals and resources for the upper elementary choir?

A.
I believe that it is important at this level to start (if you haven't already) to build a consistent and articulated music program. Ideally all students will sing and play an instrument. (National Standards 1 and 2) Recorders (song flutes) or a keyboard lab such as the Yamaha Music in Education (MIE) program are ideal at this level for teaching music fundamentals. It is essential to introduce choral skills such as PASTA (posture, air, shape, tone and articulation) at this time, as well as a sight-singing method. My favorites are listed below.

Sight-singing methods

Patterns of Sound, vol. I, II. Joyce Eilers and Emily Crocker. Hal Leonard Corporation.

Sing on Sight. Audrey Snyder. Hal Leonard Corporation.

Resources

Building Beautiful Voices. Paul Nesheim and Weston Noble. Roger Dean Publishing. An excellent source of purposeful vocal exercises.

Choir Builders. Rollo Dilworth. Hal Leonard Corporation.

Music Express Magazine. Hal Leonard Corporation. www.musicexpressmagazine.com

Music K-8 Magazine. Plank Road Publishing. www.musick8.com

Teaching Kids to Sing. Ken Phillips. Prentice Hall.
> This book is right on, comprehensive and easy to understand. There is also a set of vocal exercise cards and a video which coordinate with the book.

Musicals

If time is limited, nothing beats an all-school or grade level musical for including the most students and greatest musical reward in the shortest period of time. Again, I prefer cross-curricular presentations that reinforce units of study or important life skills. Below are a few of my favorites.

A Better You, a Better Me	Emerson	Hal Leonard
The Adventures of Lewis and Clark	Emerson/Jacobson	Hal Leonard
Bach to the Future	Gallina	Shawnee
December in Our Town	Emerson	Hal Leonard
December 'Round the World	Emerson/Jacobson	Hal Leonard
Dig It (Ancient Civilizations)	Emerson/Jacobson	Hal Leonard
The Elephant's Child (Kipling)	Jacobson/Crocker	Hal Leonard
Go West!	Emerson/Jacobson	Hal Leonard
How the West Was Really Won	Hawthorne/Wilson	Somerset
Of Mice and Mozart	Gallina	Shawnee

For a more theatrical, entertainment type of musical, check out anything by Mac Huff and John Jacobson at Hal Leonard. They are a blast and an excellent entrée into musical theater. Also, Kirby Shaw's *Jr. Jazz* series is fun and a great teaching tool.

Chorals

Any choral list is bound to reflect the musical tastes of its compiler, and the one below is no exception. I have taught all of these successfully and found that they further the goal of motivation, musical integrity, and variety. I hope you agree! All are unison or 2-part, many contain call and answer, or an ostinato for first time harmony success.

All Things Bright and Beautiful	Rutter	Fischer
Ave Verum	Mozart/Eilers	Jenson
Bashana Haba'ah	Manor/Hirsch/Leck	Hal Leonard
Bist Du Bei Mir	Bach/Bartle	Alfred
Classics for Two (Folio)	Emerson	Hal Leonard
Cripple Creek	Crocker	Hal Leonard
Dance, Dance, Dance	Donnelly/Strid	Hal Leonard
Drunken Sailor	Crocker	Hal Leonard
I Am a Small Part of the World	Albrecht	Alfred
Keep Your Hand on That Plow	Miller	Hal Leonard
Kyrie	Dwyer/Ellis/Leck	Hal Leonard
Movin' On	Hannisian	Shawnee
Nachtviolen	Schubert/Porterfield	Hal Leonard
Part Two (Folio)	Emerson	Hal Leonard
Pie Jesu	Lightfoot	Heritage
Shoshone Love Song	Emerson	Hal Leonard
Simple Gifts	Coates	Shawnee
Sing Noel	Sleeth	Hinshaw
Something Told the Wild Geese	Porterfield	Heritage
Song for a Russian Child	Klouse	Hal Leonard
Song of Peace/Dona Nobis Pacem	Donnelly/Strid	Alfred
Star Carol	Rutter	Oxford
Three Czech Folk Songs	Shaw	Hal Leonard
Ubi Caritas et Amor	Emerson	Hal Leonard
The Water is Wide	Ellen	Heritage
Wayfarin' Stranger	Emerson/Jacobson	Hal Leonard
We Want to Sing	Emerson	Hal Leonard
Where Ere You Walk	Handel/Emerson	Hal Leonard
Witness	Emerson	Hal Leonard

46

Q. Our music funding is being cutback and we may lose our program. I need some help providing rationale for the music program.

A. It is always good to be pro-active about the importance of music in your school and community. "An ounce of prevention is better than a pound of cure." Now that I am not teaching full-time, I make a concerted effort to be a music advocate for our local schools. I have used the following rationale a number of times to help justify the need for additional funding and continued support of music education.

Most state frameworks and the No Child Left Behind Act consider music "core" education. Insist that it be treated as such. It is merely tradition that places more emphasis on science and social studies. Tier 1: Reading, Writing, Basic Math. Tier 2: Science, Social Studies, Physical Education and the arts. Tier 3: Interscholastic sports and electives. Don't allow music to end up in that 3rd tier or it will be subject to cuts.

Music is a tremendously efficient program since ensembles of fifty students at a time can be taught by one instructor. Although a music program may be two hundred strong, each instructor is paid for by the ADA* of only ten students. If your district boasts "plus ada" (inter-district transfers, more in than out), it is probably because of exceptional programs such as music. These transfers may pay for the entire program!

In the case of instrumental music; parents have put up matching funds of five hundred to fifteen hundred dollars per child in the lease or purchase of instruments. The district has a fiduciary responsibility to fund and continue the program. I can think of no other subject where this is true!

Music has been shown to improve test scores (SAT) quantitatively, as reported in the MENC Journal, February, 2001. It is likely that state wide tests, such as California's API scores are also increased by a quality music program.

* average daily attendance

In smaller schools the music teacher is a lone wolf, or only teacher in their subject area, and has little clout compared to other subjects or grade levels. It is critical that you enlist parent, booster club and community support to balance this inequity. Have a group of six to twelve, credible, high profile community members on your team. Local businesses such as banks often have community grants of five hundred to one thousand dollars administered by the branch manager. Indicate the need and promotion that the bank will receive and it may be yours!

Putting on a musical production will often raise a substantial amount of money while furthering the music curriculum. Start off the year with one using student body money, and finance your music purchases for the remainder of the year.

Create a "State of the Program" report for your administrators and board so that they are aware of the scope, impact and needs of your program. Don't assume that they are aware.

A true story: I have always been sort of compulsive about organization and it has been said that I spent my high school years "organizing" concerts, dances and fundraisers through student government instead of going to class. Anyway, those skills have actually served me pretty well, particularly during my first few year of teaching. When I arrived at my first job (K-8, band, choir, general music), I was their first full-time instructor. I think the total budget had been about two hundred dollars a year and I knew right away that it needed to be a lot more. So I used those organizational skills to decide what was useable in the way of existing music and equipment, and to create a five-year plan for upgrade and replacement. Everyone thought that I was crazy to ask for two thousand dollars a year, but I made a presentation to the school board and they approved a plan for ten thousand dollars over five years! The moral of the story is, don't expect your administration to know your needs. Map out a plan and go for it. Make an effort to avoid fundraising for equipment and material needs. Save fundraising for trips and uniforms only.

Additional resources:

Dr. Tim Lautzenheiser, www.attitudeconcepts.com

47

Q. Sometimes I am criticized for performing a contemporary rock setting of a spiritual or folk song at a festival. Should I avoid these?

A. Remember that adjudicators bring their own tastes with them to the festival. I certainly would not perform more than one piece of this nature. Make sure that you perform a variety of selections; something slow and transparent, something fast and energetic and hopefully something in a foreign language.

A true story: I had been writing contemporary settings of spirituals for a few years when I was asked to present at the Iowa Choral Directors Association summer conference. Who do you think was sitting in the front row of my session but Jester Hairston! I almost went weak in the knees but continued to present my pieces. At the conclusion of the session he came up to me and gave me a big hug and said, "If only I could arrange like that!" Now realize, I think that speaks more for his graciousness than my talent, but it is still a wonderful memory. Several years later I had the opportunity to discuss the story behind the spiritual "Mary Had a Baby" with him. I had arranged this spiritual early in my career. He explained that the best time for the slaves to escape would be during the days leading up to Christmas Day, but once "Mary had her baby" the freedom train would have departed– "the train done gone." I cherish my experiences with that dear man.

48

Q. What should I do with singles of choral music that I have picked up at reading sessions? I hate to throw them away.

A. This is a Cristi Cary Miller idea: Save those pieces and when you have a few extra minutes in class, or a student who may need a little timeout, have them circle a particular element in the piece such as all of the whole notes, or quarter rests, etc. It's a win-win activity. I also like to pass on unmarked singles to other instructors at other levels or schools.

A true story: One of the first things I did when I returned to the middle school classroom was to provide a lending library for my K-4 teachers. I'm convinced that many elementary teachers enjoy including music in their classrooms when they can; they merely need the right materials. My choice was to outfit each grade level with curricular based musicals. My wife Mari and I helped them put on the first productions and from that day forward they have produced them on their own. The result is a wonderful K-4 feeder program for our 5th- 8th grade middle school, and we reap the rewards of students who come to us with singing experience.

Q. When I have auditions for a solo, no one wants to go first. Any tricks?

A. This question and answer was provided by my good friend Fred Wichmann, who followed me at the middle school. *He gives the first to audition a "do-over." Names can be pulled from a hat.* I like to do *random karaoke days* as well. This gets a lot of students singing solo who might not otherwise take the chance. You may also find some wonderful instruments in the process!

Q. Tell me something I don't know!

A. Since no one knows it all, including myself, I have distilled and included here the most important things to remember as a choir director at any level. Many we have discussed earlier in the book.

Put the singers in uniforms (T-shirts/golf shirts/vests and ties). Audiences listen with the eyes!

Space the singers elbow to elbow preferably on elevations. Make and use windows.

Provide numbered folders and music for each singer.

Sing the five common vowels (ee, eh, ah, oh, oo). Find them in every song, mark them and insist that they are sung vertically. Look at your singers especially on long notes. Use mirrors. Make a gesture that implies the shape. Try jaws down, eyebrows up.

Once parts are learned, mix the singers up or sing in the round.

Insist upon eyes on you.

Demonstrate good posture and insist that all singers use it.

Insist on silence and focus during any musical introduction or interlude.

Identify instrumentalists in your ensemble and make the link to sight-singing.

Give your singers RICE (basic rhythms, basic intervals, connect the notes, use eyes and tonal memory to remember previously sung notes).

Build choral skills (vocalize and sight-sing) at least one third of the rehearsal. Remember, the singer with the most notes (widest range) wins!

Try, and work towards conducting without music. Look your singers in the eye.

Identify and practice the three voices: chest voice, mid-voice, and head voice (root beer, milk, champagne). Avoid the chest voice, use mid-voice to A or B and then roll into head voice for notes above that.

Think the higher the note, the greater the space.

Use only a few of your best sopranos on extremely high notes.

Slightly rush and crescendo up the phrase, slow and diminuendo down.

Never leave a long note alone (either get slightly louder, softer or both).

When singing softly, shout inside!

Use a sight-singing method book five minutes or more of each rehearsal. Sight-singing empowers and engages the singer.

Cue inhalation before each and every phrase. Air is everything! Expand the rib cage at phrase endings.

Consonants give energy to the music; vowels give beauty.

Practice ballads on a neutral syllable such as "noo" or "loo." Strive for that same rich, edgeless sound when returning to the words. (Latin does this automatically for you quite well.)

Write a diction exercise on the board and point to it when the singers start to forget (usually during the second phrase!).

Do something new this year. New language, new style, a musical, add instruments, movement, bring in a resource or clinician (or a new floral piano bench cover!) etc.

Create a physical warm-up to a pop/rock song that the kids know. Start it the moment the bell rings (loud!). "YMCA" and "The Macarena" work great!

Perform a ballad in sign language.

Read the text of a song as poetry.

Explain the history of the song or current events during its composition.

Have your singers underline (in pencil) the most important words in every phrase. Sing them with a little more emphasis.

Start a special ensemble before school, during lunch or after school. (Some ideas include Chamber Choir, Jazz Choir, Show Choir, Treble Choir, Tenor/Bass Choir, Listening Club, Composition Group, etc.)

Add a treble or tenor/bass selection to your mixed choir program.

Teach as if you never have to give a concert!

Take your choir on a tour.

Record your choir during rehearsal and let them critique themselves.

Treat even the smallest group like they are special. Remember, one is a solo, two a duet, three a trio, etc.

Always provide at least one, non-select choral ensemble. The pre-requisite should be only the desire to sing!

Insist on a minimum of two, forty-minute rehearsals per week. Any less will inhibit forward momentum and continuity of skills.

Stand to sing.

Find an accompanist. You cannot maximize your skills as a conductor or retain maximum student focus behind the piano.

Mentor your feeder program.

Repertoire is your textbook! Pick it wisely.

Attend at least one conference or in-service every year.

Locate and use community resources.

Keep administration informed of your progress and your needs.

Build a parent/community advocacy group.

Be yourself! Humor goes a long way. Take what you do seriously, but not yourself.

THE NATIONAL MUSIC EDUCATION STANDARDS

1. Singing, alone and with others, a varied repertoire of music
2. Performing on instruments, alone and with others, a varied repertoire of music
3. Improvising melodies, variations and accompaniments
4. Composing and arranging music within specific guidelines
5. Reading and notating music
6. Listening to, analyzing, and describing music
7. Evaluating music and music performances
8. Understanding relationships between music, the other arts, and disciplines outside the arts
9. Understanding music in relation to history and culture

   For more on the Standards, visit the MENC website at www.menc.org

AFTERWORD

Needless to say, I have only scratched the surface of that wonderful profession that we have chosen, called choral conducting. I hope that you have picked up a point or two that will make your groups a little better. We all continue to grow with new ideas, new students and new music. I hope that you will feel free to contact me at www.rogeremerson.com if you have a question or need an idea explained. It might be fun to add your question to the sequel *Fifty More Questions to Improve Your Elementary or Middle School Choir*. I also want to encourage you to continue "doing it" in this most noble and worthy of professions. I know that we better the lives of the young people we teach because they contact us over the years with stories of how being in choir was the most memorable experience of their school years. Often times it is the student who does not stand out that is touched the most by your warmth, smile, can-do attitude and joy. Keep up the great work!

NOTES

NOTES

NOTES